More Brilliant Answers

P

PROFILE BOOKS

First published in Great Britain in 2009 by
Profile Books Ltd
3a Exmouth House
Pine Street
Exmouth Market
London EC1R 0JH
www.profilebooks.com

A CIP catalogue record for this book is available
from the British Library.

ISBN 978 1 84668 326 8

Text design by Sue Lamble
Typeset in Clarendon by MacGuru Ltd
info@macguru.org.uk

Printed and bound in the UK by
CPI Bookmarque, Croydon, CR0 4TD

contents

foreword

This is no ordinary book – and although it says AQA 63336 on the cover, really we can only claim to have written half of it.

Now you're wondering about the other half. Well, that's been written by people like you. Smart people who've had the initiative to text 63336 and ask us their imponderables.

In our five years of existence we've seen 20 million questions come and go. We're justly proud of our answers; some have even saved lives! We've had bands base songs on answers, celebs twitter that they're using us to solve family arguments, and now we're even on TV, with Auntie Beeb basing its *We Need Answers* BBC4 comedy show on our questions and answers.

We hope that sharing some jewels with you, in this, our fourth book, encourages you to stick 63336 in your phone. That way, next time you're trying to get home after staying out too late, or arguing about how many goats there are in Morocco,* you can text us, joining 2.2 million other clued-up citizens who've already asked questions.

More Brilliant Answers. Is that more answers that are brilliant, or answers that are more brilliant than any others? Both, of course.

Want to be in next year's book? Text 'BOOK' and your question to 63336 (costs £1). Get in, and you'll get a brilliant T-shirt.

---

*4.8 million, actually.

acknowledgements

After five years of answering questions, we now have more than two million customers to thank for whipping out their phones to text their important, essential and need-to-know-right-now questions to AQA 63336. It would take us 5 months, 17 days, 21 hours and 20 minutes (if we didn't sleep) to thank all of you individually, so we hope you don't mind us just saying THANK YOU here.

It is of course our researchers who are the life and blood of AQA 63336. We help them a little bit with smart algorithms, and a database full of 20 million answers, but it's the human touch, and attention to detail provided by researchers, that really makes a difference. The founders of AQA 63336 thank you for all your continuing hard work and brilliant answers.

To catch up on even more brilliant answers, go to www.aqa.63336.com.

life, sex and bodily functions

AQA 63336 knows everything, won't tell anyone what you asked, and can't blush. It's the go-to number, then, for those things you daren't ask anyone who knows you in case they go away and start making fun of you on Facebook. Let's face it, we're all pretty weird, but it's always good to know that a) your weirdnesses are actually quite interesting, and b) there's someone way, way further along the weirdness scale than you.

? what's a good dating headline that stands out for me, that's good and funny – i'm tall, pack a few extra pounds, love films, singing, kind hearted: help

> *The Tall Guy* would *Definitely, Maybe* like to meet *Little Miss Sunshine* for a bit of *Mamma Mia! In the Heat of the Night*, & hopefully some *Love Actually*.

? what happens to human hair once it has left the hairdresser's

> Hair clippings are often discarded, but can be recycled to make absorbent mats for cleaning up oil spills. The oily mats can be used to grow fungi after.

? **need technical sounding
medical terms for some
common ailments that i can
use to get off work, the
more pathetic the better**

> Hiccups are medically known as
> synchronous diaphragmatic flutters.
> A sore throat is pharyngitis. Stitch is
> exercise-related transient abdominal
> pain.

? **how much does a tear weigh
and how many tears would i
(a 34 year old male) have to
cry to lose 3 stone**

> A tear weighs 0.025g. To shed 3
> stone, you'd have to cry 760,000
> tears. Crying for an hour, you'd need
> to shed 211 tears a second. There
> there.

? what was once known as
sex in a box by its rivals 2
get it removed from shelves
in the 60s

> Denounced by competitors as 'sex in a box', Twister became a popular party game after Johnny Carson played Eva Gabor on the *Tonight Show* on 3 May 1966.

? is it possible to lick your
own forehead

> No, it is not possible to lick your own forehead. Not even Stephen Taylor, with the longest recorded tongue (9.8cm) could manage such a feat.

? in 1893 what was the first
thing to happen at the
moulin rouge

> The Moulin Rouge staged the first modern striptease on 9 February 1893. The act was a woman 'trying to find a flea' on her body. 'Ecdysiast' is the nice name for a stripper.

wot part of your body sweats the most

For most people, the feet are the sweatiest part of the body, boasting 250,000 sweat glands each and producing up to half a litre of perspiration a day.

is it possible to have your appendix removed through your mouth

Yes, it is possible to have the appendix removed via the mouth. The first such operation was carried out on 12 March 2008 in San Diego, California.

there is a fragrance for men, and it was made with bulbs and ballpoint pen – what is it called

Odeur 71 by Des Garcons, for men and women, captures the scent of dust from a hot light bulb, metal, lettuce, pen ink, pencil shavings, a toaster and wood.

? why does the aborigine in the movie australia stand on one leg

Apart from conserving energy, Aborigines stand on one leg as it helps them hunt for food more efficiently: their shadow appears tree-like.

? how many people in the world are blind physically

Globally, more than 161 million people are visually impaired, of whom 124 million people have low vision and 37 million are blind.

? what is schweffing

'Schweffing' is when someone should be drinking with his or her friends, yet can be found in the corner slyly chatting up a member of the opposite sex.

? did legendary cartoonist walt disney have himself frozen, with the hope of returning later on when a cure for what killed him has been found

> Walt Disney wasn't frozen after he died. He was cremated on 17 December 1966. James Bedford became the first human to be cryogenically preserved, on 12 January 1967.

? are only humans self conscious

> Humans are not the only self-conscious animals. Scientific research has shown that bottlenose dolphins, elephants and some apes also have self-awareness.

? for an average medium size tank top how many pubic hairs will one need

> You'd need 28 million pubic hairs to knit a tank top – the hairs would need to be spun together to make a yarn. It would be washable on a wool setting.

? how much water vapour is generated by a human being in 24 hours

Humans typically release 1.2l of water vapour a day – 300ml is exhaled and 900ml is lost through the skin. A further 1.5l of water is produced as urine.

? how many peas could i fit in my head if i hollowed out my skull, and how many baked beans are in the tin

If you hollowed out your skull, you would be able to fit 3,200 peas into it. There are 215 baked beans in one tin. The human skull has 22 bones.

? is there anything wrong with eating nose mucus

Nose-picking and nasal mucus eating provoke disgust when done in public. However, some doctors claim it benefits the immune system, so it's not wrong.

how do you make love stay

You make love stay by working at it.
Love is like a tomato ketchup bottle;
it looks very full from the outside, but
it takes work to get anything out.

what is the average waist line of both males and females in america

In America, the average male waist
size is 39in and the average waist size
for a woman is 36.5in. The Statue of
Liberty's waistline measures a curvy
34ft 9in.

how long would it take to grow hair as long as the m3

It'd take 628,667 years to grow your
hair 94.3km long – the M3's length.
The Woodstock Festival could be held,
like, 73,478,599 times as you did it,
man.

world's most tattooed person has what percentage of his body tattooed

Lucky Diamond Rich is the most tattooed person in the world. 100% of his body is covered in black ink, even his eyelids, inner ears and between his toes.

which european country is it where people with red hair are said to bring bad luck

Redheads are considered bad luck in Corsica. In Denmark, it's an honour to have a redheaded child. Bees are thought to sting redheads more than others.

what's the longest fit of laughter that's ever been recorded

The Tanganyika laughter epidemic began on 30 January 1962 and lasted for six months. 1,000 people suffered the mass hysteria; no medical cause existed.

how wide are the largest stretched ear lobes

The largest stretched earlobes are a massive 5.5in in diameter, sported by body modification legend 'Bear'. He recently had his nipples pierced too.

how long do i need to have sex to burn off a 12" pizza

Having sex uses 5 calories per minute. A 12-inch pizza has around 2,000 calories so it would take you 400 minutes, or 6 hours and 40 minutes, to burn it off.

who has the largest feet at present

The Marco Shoe Factory in Ukraine make the world's biggest shoes to fit Leonid Stadnyk's size 27 feet (17in). He's a qualified vet and is 8ft 4in tall.

? is the statue of liberty naked underneath her clothes

The Statue of Liberty is not only not naked under her robes, she has no body. The statue is on a framework of steel, and used to be accessible to the public.

? what's the ratio of toilets to people in the uk

There are 0.92 toilets per person in the UK. That's 56 million loos for 61 million people, so if everyone has to go at the same time, we're in trouble.

? what does tricophage mean

Trichophagia is the term given to the compulsive eating of hair. Long hair is often chewed while still attached to the head and then swallowed.

? on average, how much per year does a woman spend on bras

UK women spend £60 a year each on bras but many wash them only 6 times a year. The UK bra industry is worth £39 billion. 55% of all bras sold are white.

? how did the vikings cut their hair, nails, nose hair and brush their teeth

Vikings had scissors (called snips) and tweezers for hair, nose and nails. They used twigs on their teeth and filed them. Christians thought them over-clean.

? when did women begin to get rid of the hair on their legs and armpits

Women began removing their body hair as far back as 4000 BC. They applied creams containing arsenic, quicklime and starch – not recommended nowadays.

? are there any statistics on percentage of women who diet/try to lose weight for their wedding day

70% of women attempt to lose weight before their wedding. One in seven brides-to-be buys a gown that is at least one size smaller than they'd normally wear.

? is it true that if you unwrap your brain it is the same length around as the earth

A brain contains 164,600km of nerve fibres. The Earth's circumference is 40,076km, so an unwrapped brain would actually stretch 4 times around the Earth.

? how many human hairs in the world

There are 33,917,127,635,567,000 human hairs in the world. Only 2% of adult hair is found on the head. People shed up to 100 hairs a day.

? would i be able to put a bet on that my nan will live to 100

Yes, you can place a bet that your nan will live to 100. In 2004, Jennifer Strover received £12,500 after betting her mother-in-law would live to 100.

? has anyone ever died from laughter

Yes. In the 3rd century BC, the Greek philosopher Chrysippus died of laughter after giving his donkey wine and then watching it try to eat figs. Hilarious.

? wat wld b the repercussions of belly flopping off the dartford crossing bridge into the river thames

You would die. The bridge is 65 metres high. Belly flopping from 15 metres or higher is fatal. The world record belly flop was from 10.6 metres.

what happened to a vestal virgin when she broke her vow of chastity

If a Vestal Virgin broke her vow of celibacy, she would be buried alive in the Campus Sceleratus in Rome. Sex with a citizen was seen as incest and treason.

nowadays are more children born to people in their 20s or 30s in the uk

More children are born to mothers in the 20–29 (50% births) than 30–39 (40% births) age bracket. In five-year groups, 20–24 is the most fertile age.

can food go down the wrong way?

Food can indeed 'go down the wrong way'. It can go into the lungs, causing coughing and choking, and in severe cases, chest infections and pneumonia.

in which country do people lose their virginity the earliest, and which the latest

On average, people in Iceland lose their virginity the earliest, at 15.6 years of age. People wait the longest in India, at 19.8 years. World average is 17.3.

how many erections does a man have

The average man has 11 erections per day, 9 of them asleep. On average, a man will have spent three years of his life with an erect penis.

why do we have 2 nostrils

We have two nostrils because we're bilaterally symmetrical, having evolved from sea sponges. It's useful, as if one is blocked or damaged, we can still breathe.

? do you get paid for donating sperm

> When donating sperm, you can be compensated for loss of earnings up to a daily maximum of £55.19. This is capped at £250 per course of sperm donation.

? is it possible to determine the difference between a fake tear and a real emotional tear

> Yes. Emotional tears contain markedly more hormones and natural painkillers (such as prolactin and leucine enkephalin) than tears produced by other means.

? are there any geniuses who were neat & tidy & organised

> Genius physicist and engineer Nikola Tesla was obsessively clean and tidy. He wouldn't touch anything dirty, or anything round, and used 18 napkins per meal.

eat to live, live to eat

One reason why the human race is still going is that we don't put any old thing in our mouths without asking a few questions first. AQA 63336 is delighted to be able to give a helping hand to evolution by informing the ravenous and warning the hasty. Today's specials include piping shrike, well-done slugs, and 12,187 tonnes of cheese, with a wally on the side. Still hungry? There are 1 billion After Eights to pass round. Go on.

? how long would a chocolate fireguard take to melt if it was placed in front of a fire

A chocolate fireguard would take two hours to melt into a pool on the hearth. A chocolate teapot would melt within 3min 40sec of being filled with boiling water.

? which country eats the most easter eggs per head

Australians are the world's largest consumers of Easter eggs. Each year, they consume an average of 10 eggs per person – that's over 200 million eggs.

? where did the drink 'punch' originally come from

Punch comes from India, where it was a drink with five ingredients – arrack, sugar, lemon, water and tea. 'Punch' comes from 'panch', meaning 'five' in Hindi.

? **who was the first person on record to cook food in boiling water**

Huou, court chef for Kublai Khan (1215–94), had the first recipe involving boiling, in his book *The Important Things to Know About Eating and Drinking*.

? **monks in austria believe that by doing what their cheese turns into a prize winner**

An Austrian school for dairy farmers claims that chanting by monks produces prize-winning cheese. They play it on a loop as the cheese matures in cellars.

? **what is the highest restaurant in europe**

Le 3842 in Chamonix, in the Alps, is the highest restaurant in Europe in terms of altitude. The furthest from the ground is Le Ciel de Paris, in Paris.

? is human spit used to ferment beer in africa or elsewhere

> African palm beer and Andean chicha use spit to aid fermentation, as did rice ale in ancient China. Spit converts starch to sugar, making the beer sweeter.

? what are ortolans

> Ortolans are tiny songbirds which were a French delicacy until a law banned eating them in 1999. They were drowned in brandy, roasted for 8 minutes and eaten whole.

? if i were to try and swim in tomato ketchup, would i be able to or would i drown

> You can swim in tomato ketchup without drowning, but only if you are actually able to swim. Non-swimmers should learn in water and build up to condiments.

? where in the bible does it prohibit the consumption of pork and shellfish

It is forbidden to eat pork and shellfish in Leviticus 11:7–12. Camels, ospreys, ferrets, chameleons, bats, snails, moles and owls are also forbidden.

? what was on the front of a bottle of heinz tomato ketchup b4 the tomato

A pickled gherkin graced the Heinz tomato ketchup bottle until January 2009. In a shock move, the company replaced the 114-year-old pickle with a tomato.

? how do u spell that bowl with handles that u drink whisky out of made of silver or pewter

A quaich is a small whisky cup, usually made from silver. It has two handles. The word quaich is from the Gealic word 'cuach', meaning shallow cup.

which is the bigger selling brand in america, coca-cola or pepsi

Across the USA and the world, Coca-Cola outsells Pepsi. Pepsi is more popular in India, while local cola brands outsell both in Turkey, Slovenia and Peru.

when were after eights invented

After Eight mints were invented by the Rowntree Company in 1962. Nestle have made them since 1988. 1bn are made annually, each containing 28 calories.

where did people go in london to breathe in their drinks

Alcoholic Architecture was a London bar in which the air was saturated with gin and tonic, so patrons could breathe the cocktail. It was open for one week.

what did britain eat during the beef shortage in 1951

Due to shortage of beef, Britain consumed 53,000 horses for food in 1951. Meat was rationed to just four ounces of rump steak per person per week.

what's smellier than an anchovy

Far smellier than an anchovy is titan arum, the world's smelliest plant, stinking of rotting flesh. Don't use in a bouquet, unless you want to break up.

what meats do u have to eat from the ozzie coat of arms

If eating the Australian coat of arms, you'd chew on kangaroo and emu, with a side of piping shrike, swan, and lion (red and gold).

? why does lager froth when salt is poured into it

In any fizzy drink, CO_2 bubbles continually try to form, but need 'nucleation sites' to form at. Salt grains provide thousands of these sites in one go.

? what marched to london from norfolk just before christmas each year

In the Victorian era, turkeys were walked the 80 miles from Norfolk to London markets for Christmas. They set out in October and wore little leather boots.

? how much rice is grown in japan each year

Japan grows over 11 million tons of rice each year, most of which is used domestically. The US produces 100 million tons, whilst China grows 185 million.

what do you call it when you cut a melon in a serrated fashion

A 'Van Dyked' melon has the zig-zag edges, as seen at 1970s dinner parties. Melons are grown in glass cubes in Japan for easy stacking in the fridge.

how many jelly beans does the jelly belly candy company make in one hour

Jelly Belly makes 1,249,200 jelly beans an hour. The name was inspired by Leadbelly, a 1920s blues singer. They were the first jelly beans in space.

who is the joanna that cockburn's 1967 joanna port is named after – thanks

Joanna's Port is named after a Joanna who received 600 bottles of relabelled 1967 Cockburn's for her 21st birthday, but sold most bottles on to resellers.

? what is eaten for dessert in sweden at christmas

Julgrot is a traditional dessert served at Christmas in Sweden. It's a rice pudding with one or more whole almonds inside, and whoever finds one will marry.

? where did the arabic dessert omali originate from

Legend has it that the Arabic Om Ali dessert is named after its creator, the wife of Sultan Ezz El Din Aybek. It's made with filo pastry and nuts.

? what food product was banned in canada from 1886 until 1949

Margarine was banned in Canada between 1886 and 1949. WWI shortages meant the ban was lifted from 1917 to 1923. Napoleon III paid for margarine's invention.

❓ was mr potato actually a real potato

Mr Potato Head was originally launched in 1952, as body parts to use on a real potato. A plastic body was added in 1964, and variations were added later.

❓ does gin go off

No, gin doesn't go off. In the 18th century, gin used to be flavoured with sulphuric acid and turpentine. Nowadays, juniper berries give it its taste.

❓ is there mash potato in ice cream

No, there's no mashed potato in ice cream. However, when ice cream is advertised, mashed potato will often be used for the photos to avoid melting due to hot lighting.

what's the biggest round of drinks ever bought

In 2001, a German fruit importer spent a record £42,608.25 on a round of drinks in London. It included 40 bottles of Cristal champagne and 20 bottles of Bollinger.

what food never goes off

Salt, sugar and vinegar are the three foods which never go off. Under UK legislation they do not need to be marked with a 'best before end' date.

can you eat slugs

Slugs are edible. However, they contain the parasite Angiostrongylus cantonensis, potentially causing meningitis if inadequately cooked or eaten raw.

what are the 5 oldest breweries in england in order

The five oldest breweries, still operating, in England are: Young's (1581); Shepherd Neame (1698); Samuel Smith (1758); Courage & Co (1787) and Greene King (1799).

？ approx how many grammes of coffee does a coffee tree produce on average per season

The average coffee bush produces 900g of coffee beans every year, which is enough to make 50–60 decent cups of ground coffee, or 120 cups of instant.

？ what was the best thing before sliced bread

The best thing before sliced bread was unsliced bread. The two are similar, but the convenience of sliced when one fancies a lazy lunch cannot be overstated.

？ what is the name of the measure of beer less than half a pint i think normally 0.3 pints

The name for a measure of a beer which is a third of a pint is a 'nip'. It's common at beer festivals, so as to let attendees try lots of different ales.

what's the world chilli-eating record

The record for eating the world's hottest chili, Naga Jolokia, is held by a 26-year-old Indian woman, Anandita Dutta Tamuly. She ate 51 in 2 minutes in 2009.

which english beer has the highest alcohol content

The strongest beer in the UK is Domesday II by Devenish (15.9%). The strongest in the world is Sam Adams Utopia MMII at 24%, brewed by Boston Beer Co.

what is the british record for the heaviest show onion

The UK's (and the world's) heaviest show onion weighed 16lb 8.5oz. It was grown by John Sifford from Bromsley, West Midlands, in 2005. He won £1,500.

how much cheese does america eat every day

The USA devours 12,187 tonnes of cheese every day, requiring the daily milk of 2,229,258 cows. Mozzarella is the nation's favourite, followed by cheddar.

when and where was the first restaurant in the world opened

The world's first restaurant was in Kaifeng, China, in the 11th century. The word restaurant first applied to Boulanger's, which opened in Paris in 1765.

how much is the most expensive pie in the world

The world's most expensive pie cost £8,000. It was made with two bottles of 1982 Chateau Mouton Rothschild , rare Chinese mushrooms and Japanese wagyu beef.

? do you think in an average bloke's lifetime starting from the age of 18 he could have a pint in every pub in britain

There are 59,000 pubs in the UK. An 18-year-old having 2 pints a day in different pubs would need to live to 99 to drink one in each (72 for 3 pints a day).

? can veg talk

Vegetables cannot 'talk' as such, but injured tomato plants do communicate with other plants by releasing a chemical warning signal into the air.

? what weight of raw popcorn kernels would be needed to feed 2,000 people a small/med sized portion

You'd need about 85kg (188lb) of corn kernels to feed 2,000 people with popcorn. The Aztecs believed the popping sound was made by angry gods escaping.

the sound
of music

We share 98% of our DNA with chimpanzees. Clearly, within that 2% is the noisy little molecule that makes us want to hit drums, strum lutes, blow bagpipes and buy iPods. AQA 63336 does to your phone what rock 'n' roll did to a pleasant Saturday tea-dance, and you don't even have to take out your earphones to text us a question.

? **have sales of cherry chapstick gone up as a result of i kissed a girl**

Sales of cherry Chapstick have gone through the roof since the release of Katy Perry's 'I Kissed A Girl'. Three-tube value packs have been released in America.

? **when will now that's what i call music 100 album be released**

At the moment, three *Now!* albums are released every year – for Easter, July and Christmas. *Now 100!* will be released in July 2018, all being well.

? **what was the last non x factor winner christmas no 1 and when was it, and have any x factor winners not got to no 1**

The last non-*X Factor* Christmas No. 1 was in 2004 when Band Aid 20 were No. 1 for 4 weeks. Every *X Factor* winner has had a debut No. 1 single.

how many classic les paul guitars would it take to cover the whole of america and then give one to every born and bred american

To cover the whole of the USA with Classic Les Paul guitars would use 32,800,000,000,000 of them, 107,432 for each American. Cost: $32.8 billion billion.

1st pm to make a sound recording

On 18 December 1888, William Gladstone became the first Prime Minister to be recorded, on wax cylinder. William Edison invented the phonograph in 1877.

name some songs that have names of fish in their title or bands with fish names in their name

Songs: 'The Salmon Dance', 'Addicted to Bass', 'Angel Eyes', 'Ray of Light', 'Tears of a Clown', 'O For'tuna'. Bands: Eels, The Seahorses, Hootie & The Blowfish, The Carp-enters.

rolf harris can produce this vocal sound which goes um ca ha, do you know what it is called

Rolf Harris's trademark vocalisation is known as 'eefing' and originated in rural Tennessee in the 19th century. It was popularised by Jimmy Riddle.

what was the 1000th song to reach number 1 in the uk

Elvis Presley's 'One Night' became the 1,000th song to reach No. 1 on 22 January 2005. It was his 20th UK No. 1 and had previously charted in January 1959.

in the 12 days of christmas, what were 'the 4 calling birds'

'Calling birds', in the '12 Days' song, is derived from the original term 'colly bird'. 'Colly' means black. Therefore, the line is about blackbirds.

? **why is everyone wearing pink carnations in the orchestra on the last night of the proms**

Carnations are worn as a buttonhole on the Last Night of the Proms in memory of the Proms' founder, Sir Henry Wood. He always wore one when conducting.

? **which is the only song during ww2 that was sung by both allied and axis troops**

In WW2, the troops of both sides were fond of singing 'Lili Marlene'. Its most famous singer is Marlene Dietrich, who recorded it in both German and English.

? **where did 10cc's name come from**

Jonathan King named 10cc. Band member Lol Creme said it referred to one better than the 9cc of semen in an average ejaculation, but Kevin Godley denies it.

which bob dylan song has the highest number of words in it

'Lily, Rosemary and the Jack Of Hearts' contains 954 words, split over 16 verses – more than any other Bob Dylan song. It's from *Blood on the Tracks*.

what was midnight train to georgia by gladys night called originally

'Midnight Train to Georgia' was originally called 'Midnight Train to Houston'. Cissy Houston (Whitney's mum) was asked to record it, so the name was changed.

wot is the only song to get to christmas number 1 with no music in it

'Only You' by The Flying Pickets is the only song to have become a Christmas No. 1 without using music. It was sung 'a cappella' and was a hit in 1983.

in what year did radio 1 stop announcing the new single chart on tuesday lunch time

> Radio 1 announced the new singles chart on a Tuesday lunchtime for the last time on 29 September 1987. It moved to Sunday afternoons on 4 October 1987.

what is the highest position ever obtained in the uk singles chart by a cumbrian band

> 'Calling All the Heroes' by It Bites got to No. 6 in 1986, the highest-ever for an all-Cumbrian band. 911's Lee Brennan is the only Cumbrian to get to No. 1.

how much did the beatles sign their 1st contract for

> The Beatles' first contract was for 1d per record sold. Brian Epstein would take 25% if they sold over £200 a week, 20% if £100–200, or 15% if under £100.

? what supermarket is mentioned in the song a town called malice

The Co-op is mentioned in 'Town Called Malice' by The Jam. The line is 'A whole street's belief in Sunday's roast beef, gets dashed against the Co-op'.

? in the song i'm not in love by 10cc who is the female voice who speaks

The female voice that whispers 'Be quiet, big boys don't cry' in the song 'I'm Not in Love' by 10cc belonged to the secretary of Strawberry Studios, Kathy Redfern.

? did the rolling stones ever play in rhyl or prestatyn

The Rolling Stones' first ever gig outside England was at the Royal Lido Ballroom, Prestatyn, on 31 August 1963. A week later, they appeared in Aberystwyth.

where is the long and winding road

Paul McCartney said 'The Long and Winding Road' was inspired by the 31-mile stretch of the B842 from Kintyre to Campbeltown, near his farm in Scotland.

how did oasis get their name

Liam Gallagher suggested Oasis after seeing a picture of Swindon's Oasis Leisure Centre on an Inspiral Carpets tour poster. Before this, they were The Rain.

what song has coco bean in it

'Love In The First Degree' by Bananarama has the lyric 'Guilty! Guilty as a girl can be' – commonly misheard as 'Guilty! Guilty as a cocoa bean.'

where does the stone roses' name come from

The Stone Roses named themselves after a 1959 spy thriller novel by Sarah Gainham (1915–99). Guitarist John Squire owned a copy of the book.

what were the crickets known as before buddy came along

The Crickets were known as The Three Tunes before they started playing with Buddy Holly. They considered calling themselves The Beetles.

what was keith richards record for staying awake

Keith Richards' record for staying awake is 9 days in a row in the 1970s. On the last day, he fell asleep so suddenly that he broke his nose on a speaker.

infamy – the world of celebrity

Famous people are a bit like penguins. We never tire of watching their endearing and peculiar antics (and they can't fly). On second thoughts, they tend not to get buckets of fish thrown at them, and a good thing too. Still, these special forms of humanity provoke endless questions. Such as, when they're having their hair done, do they read magazines full of photos of normal people?

? with what does catherine zeta jones say she brushes her teeth

Catherine Zeta-Jones says she uses strawberry pulp to clean her teeth. It contains malic acid, which acts as an astringent and can lighten surface stains.

? what's the pantone reference for dale winton

Dale Winton's skin tone closely matches Pantone 167 C, a warm mix of orange and brown. The first colour-matching system was developed in 1963.

? what was noah's wife called

Noah's wife is not named in the Bible, but according to Jewish tradition her name was Naamah. 10% of Americans think Joan of Arc was Noah's wife.

? **is it true that will smith can do the rubiks cube quikley**

Yes, Will Smith learned to solve Rubik's Cube for *The Pursuit of Happyness*, achieving 55 seconds. Erik Akkersdijk holds the world record: 7.08 seconds.

? **what links kate moss and arne schwarznegar**

Kate Moss and Arnold Schwarzenegger both own a London black cab, as do Stephen Fry and Prince Philip. The late Stanley Kubrick also used to own one.

? **which actor claims he was partially responsible for the destruction of the berlin wall**

David Hasselhoff claims he helped the fall of the Berlin Wall. He feels he reunited Germany when he sang 'Looking For Freedom' in Berlin in 1989.

? is it true bono once paid for a first class seat in an airplane to fly one of his hats

> In 2003, Bono flew his trilby hat first class from Gatwick to Bologna at a cost of £442. He also paid £100 (including tip) for a cab to get it to Gatwick.

? how can i make russell brand fall in love with me

> Russell Brand has described his ideal woman as 'Sensitive, funny and sweet. Like a poem or a cloud'. To win his love, practise being a poem or cloud.

? who was the teen girl progidy to say i love my calvins

> In 1980, Brooke Shields, 15, declared 'You want to know what comes between me and my Calvins? Nothing.' She dated Michael Jackson briefly when she was 18.

where does the word 'papparazsy' as in press people, come from

The word paparazzi is derived from the name of the character Paparazzo in Federico Fellini's *La Dolce Vita*. The word is Italian for an annoying noise.

how old was charlie chaplin when he had his last child

Charlie Chaplin was 73 years old when he had his last child, Christopher James Chaplin (born 8 July 1962). Chaplin had 11 children, between 1919 and 1962.

which royal was slapped with flowers in latvia

Alina Lebedeva slapped Prince Charles in the face with a flower in Latvia on 8 November 2001. She was protesting over Britain's involvement in Afghanistan.

any celebs ever been hijacked

Greek singer Demis Roussos was one of the passengers on hijacked TWA flight 847 in 1985. The hijackers celebrated his 39th birthday with him on board.

what are the secret service code names for president obama his family and vice president biden

Barack Obama's Secret Service code name is Renegade. Michelle's is Renaissance and their daughters are Rosebud and Radiance. Joe Biden is known as Celtic.

name hollywood actors who can fly planes

Actors who hold a pilot's licence: John Travolta, Clint Eastwood, Morgan Freeman, Kris Kristofferson, Dennis Quaid, Harrison Ford, Tom Cruise, Patrick Swayze, Kurt Russell, Cliff Robertson, Fess Parker (who played Davy Crockett), Michael Dorn (Worf in Star Trek) and Angelina Jolie.

❓ whose stats are 40–27–37

Dolly Parton's stats are a remarkable 40–27–37. She is 5ft tall. If Barbie were life-sized, her stats would be 36–13–38 and she would be 7ft 2in tall.

❓ what city has norman wisdom been given freedom to

Norman Wisdom was awarded the freedom of Tirana, Albania's capital, in 1995. His films were the only Western films allowed during Enver Hoxha's dictatorship.

❓ did cher remove her bottom two ribs to give her a smaller waist

Cher didn't have ribs removed. Her wasp waist is kept in shape by working out. But she's had a face lift, nose job, breast augmentation and dental braces.

? what new york gangster helped the american army in the 2nd world war, from jail

Charles 'Lucky' Luciano, whilst in Clinton County Jail in 1943, used his connections with the Sicilian Mafia to assist the Allies in invading Italy.

? who was the first monarch to use the telephone

Queen Victoria was the first monarch to use the telephone. Alexander Graham Bell demonstrated it to her on 14 January 1878, but she was not impressed.

? in a poll of dead people this person tops a list of top earners who earned 35 millions dollars last year

Elvis Presley is the highest earning dead celebrity. Last year he earned a whopping $52m (£36.5m). Charles M. Schulz was second on the list, earning $33m.

? who would win in a fight: barry from chucklevision or timmy mallett

> Timmy Mallett would win in a fight against Barry Chuckle. Timmy has youth and Mallett's Mallet on his side. He would also blind Barry with his shirt.

? writer named after a lake in staffs, english

> English writer and Nobel Prize winner Rudyard Kipling was named after Rudyard Lake, a reservoir in Rudyard, Staffordshire. His parents met there in 1863.

? how much does it cost to hire kylie for about 5 mins, just enough time for her to make a cup of tea and sing i should be so lucky

> It would cost £166,665 to hire Kylie Minogue for five minutes, based on her rates for a Dubai opening ceremony, where she earned £1.5m for 10 songs.

? kiki hankinson achieved what in 1951

Kiki Hakansson was the winner of the first Miss World pageant, which took place in 1951. She represented Sweden, and was the only woman to don a bikini.

? was lee marvin in the army

Lee Marvin was a US Marine Corps sniper during WWII. He was shot in the buttocks during the Battle of Saipan, and received a Purple Heart for his injury.

? who has more money, paris hilton or lisa marie presley

Lisa Marie Presley has more money than Paris Hilton. She inherited her father's $100m fortune. Paris is waiting to inherit $5m to add to her own assets.

❓ was actor andy garcia born as a siamese twin

Andy Garcia was born with an undeveloped conjoined twin attached to his shoulder. It was about the size of a tennis ball, and was surgically removed.

❓ which actress had a lion called winston churchill

US actress Tallulah Bankhead had a pet lion called Winston Churchill and a monkey called King Kong. She famously said 'I am as pure as the driven slush.'

❓ what's mia farrow's sister called

Mia Farrow's sister is named Prudence. She is the subject of the song 'Dear Prudence' by The Beatles, written when John Lennon met her in India.

? does every new american president swear on abraham lincoln's bible

No, Barack Obama was the first US president to be sworn in using Abraham Lincoln's Bible since Lincoln used it in 1861. George W. Bush used a family Bible.

? which magazine did shane ritchie sells photo rights of his 40th birthday to for £1.10

In 2004 Shane Richie sold the rights of his 40th birthday to *The Big Issue* for £1.10. He turned down a £150,000 offer from a high profile magazine.

? who was the exception to the rule of no living person to appear on british postage stamps

Roger Taylor, the Queen drummer, is the only non-Royal living person to appear on a British stamp. He was in the background of a Freddie Mercury stamp.

can you find what person appears three times on the cover of the beatles' sgt peppers lonely hearts club band

Shirley Temple's image appears three times on the cover of The Beatles' 1967 album *Sgt. Pepper's Lonely Hearts Club Band* (two photos and a doll in her image).

wot news reader is donating his brain 2 medical science

Jeremy Paxman is donating his brain to medical science once he dies, to help Parkinson's disease research. It affects around 1 in 500 people in the UK.

what happened to henry the 8th's body at his funeral

While Henry VIII, entombed in a lead coffin, was being transported to Windsor for burial, his casket started to come apart, leaking his bodily fluids.

? **has the queen of england
ever gone to a pub**

> Yes, Queen Elizabeth II visited the
> Bridge Inn, Topsham, Devon in 1998.
> She accepted a case of ale for Prince
> Philip, but didn't partake in a tipple.

? **are winston churchill and
princess diana related**

> Yes, Winston Churchill and Princess
> Diana (and ex-President Bush) are
> distant relatives. Their ancestry can
> be traced back to Henry Spencer of
> Badby, 1420–78.

? **who had their teeth insured
for 1m pounds in the 70s**

> Ken Dodd insured his teeth for £4
> million in the 1970s. He gained his
> famous buck-toothed smile after a
> nasty bicycle accident when he was 7
> years old.

athletic and sporting endeavours

If the mountains of statistics weren't reason enough to love the world of competitive games, it also rewards our faithful fandom with calamitous collisions, nail-biting dramas and, of course, the endlessly pleasing sight of buff bodies thundering around fields and powering through pools. It's a trigger for national pride and national gloom, especially when the surprising or corrupt happens. And as this trophy cabinet of questions and answers shows, all the rule books, umpires, whistles, penalties and sin bins in the world can't keep the unexpected – and the underhand – out of sport.

？ has a man ever bet his car or house on a football game

On 29 September 2001, to impress his girlfriend, a fan bet his entire mortgage on Tottenham beating Man United when they led 3–0 at half time. They lost 5–3.

？ how many competitors did the first motor race attract

The first motor race, held in Paris on 28 April 1887, attracted only one competitor, Georges Bouton. Not surprisingly, he won the 2km race.

？ who is the strangest olympic medallist ever

The strangest Olympic medallist ever was the mad Emperor Nero who competed in the AD 67 chariot race and introduced new musical events, winning gold in all.

what team does bin laden support

Osama Bin Laden is an Arsenal fan. He was observed at Arsenal games in the 1990s. He became interested in football whilst growing up in the Middle East.

has anyone ever cheated (and then been disqualified) at the tour de france by taking the train

In 1904, Maurice Garin was disqualified from the Tour de France for taking the train. He had won the year before, without the need for public transport.

he scored for newcastle and saved a penalty for man utd

In a Sugar Puffs advert, the Honey Monster scored for Newcastle and saved a penalty for Manchester United, having replaced an injured Peter Schmeichel.

how fast does a golf club head travel when it is swung

A regular golfer swings a golf club at 77–95mph. A tour pro will swing a club at 110–127mph and long drive professionals swing from 135 to 145mph.

how many minutes did bobby moore play for england

Bobby Moore played every minute of each of his 108 England caps – 9,780 in total. This included two 30-minute periods of extra time against West Germany.

when hagler beat hearns in three rounds, how many punches were thrown in the first round

165 punches were thrown in the 1st round of Hagler vs Hearns in 1985 – 82 by Hagler, 83 by Hearns. Remarkably, 106 of these punches landed.

? why is astroturf called astroturf please

Chemgrass was renamed AstroTurf by John Wortmann after its first high-profile use at the Houston Astrodome stadium in 1966. It was patented a year later.

? first player to be disqualified at wimbledon

In 1995, Tim Henman was the first player to be disqualified at Wimbledon. He hit a ball in anger, accidentally clonking ballgirl Caroline Hall's head.

? wot team has been in the top flight for 70yrs and never won the league

Bolton have spent 70 non-consecutive seasons in the top flight of English football without winning the title. They've won the FA Cup four times, though.

what was the first ever world record for the 100 metre sprint

Don Lippincott set the first official men's 100m world record, at 10.6sec on 6 July 1912, in the heats of the Stockholm Olympics. He was third in the final.

who was the first player to play for england that never played for an english team

In 1959, Hibernian's Joe Baker became the first player to win an England cap without playing for an English club; Owen Hargreaves was the second (in 2001).

who was the 1st country to win elephant polo

James Manclark's Scottish team were the first world champions of elephant polo, in 1982. England won in December 2008. Each tournament uses 16 elephants.

? did ali fight a wrestler

> Muhammad Ali (Cassius Clay) fought wrestler Antonio Inoki in a wrestler vs boxer match in Tokyo, Japan on 26 June 1976. The match was declared a draw.

? has the ball ever burst in a major football cup

> In both the 1946 and 1947 FA Cup finals the ball burst during the game. Charlton Athletic played in both finals, losing in 1946 and winning in 1947.

? why did only some of the tottenham players' jerseys have a sponsor on them in the 1987 fa cup final

> In the 1987 FA Cup final, due to a mistake at Hummell's factory, only half of the Tottenham shirts had the sponsor's name Holsten printed on them.

? how much did china spend on the olympics and how much was the opening ceremony

Officially, the 2008 Beijing Olympics cost £15bn (on a par with Athens 2004), but the full costs are a record £40bn. The opening ceremony cost £150m.

? ex everton player that was hung in australia

It's alleged that ex-Everton player Alexander 'Sandy' Young was hanged for sheep rustling in Australia. He scored the only goal in the 1906 FA Cup final.

? when was table tennis invented

Table tennis was invented in England in 1880. It began with Cambridge University students using lids from cigar boxes and rounded champagne corks.

? **which team has appeared in the most fa cup finals without winning**

Leicester City have appeared in the most FA Cup finals without winning; a heartbreaking four times. Scottish club Queen's Park appeared twice in the final.

? **name given for a person who makes cricket bats**

A pod crafter makes (or shaves) cricket bats. 90% of the willow used worldwide for cricket bats comes from J. S. Wright & Sons in Chelmsford.

? **which player has been an unused substitute the most times in premiership history**

Newcastle goalie Steve Harper has been an unused Premier League substitute a record 272 times. He played in the 1999 FA Cup final, but they lost 2–0.

? which football team in england have been relegated the most times

Notts County have been relegated 15 times in their history – more than any other league club. Arsenal have had the fewest relegations, with one.

? has there ever been an olympic winner with a pacemaker

Pacemakers (aka rabbits) aren't used in the athletics. Olympic shooter Bret Erickson has an artificial pacemaker fitted to his heart, but hasn't won.

? how many people, if any, have completed all the london marathons

There are 22 people who've finished every London Marathon since its 1981 inception. Known as 'Ever Presents', all 22 are men. The eldest is 74 years old.

?how many 147 breaks have there been at the crucible and who got them

There have been nine 147 breaks at the Crucible: Thorburn (1983), White (1992), Hendry (1995 and 2009), O'Sullivan (1997, 2003 and 2008), Williams (2005) and Ali Carter (2008).

?david frost was selected for which major football team

Sir David Frost turned down a contract with Nottingham Forest FC in order to attend Cambridge University. He graduated with an honours degree in English.

?2 sports you can use spoons in

The two sports in which you would use a spoon are angling and rowing. A spoon is a type of lure used in angling and is a term for the blade of an oar in rowing.

which was the first football club to be founded outside england

The first football club to be founded outside England was Lausanne Football & Cricket Club in Switzerland in 1860. It was founded by English students.

what is a thunderer

The ACME Thunderer is the most common whistle used by football referees. It was invented by Joseph Hudson in 1884. It works in the rain.

what is the highest score by any team in 2020 cricket

The highest ever Twenty20 innings is a mammoth 366/3 by Austerlands vs Droylsden. The highest in an international is Sri Lanka's 260/6 vs Kenya in 2007.

what's the record for the quickest goal scored ever

The fastest ever goal was 2.5 seconds, scored by the late Marc Burrows for Cowes Sports against Eastleigh in a Wessex League match on 3 April 2004.

worst footballing accident in the premiership

The worst Premiership accident was David Busst's broken leg against Man United in 1996. Peter Schmeichel vomited and required counselling after seeing it.

what has the arch at wembley stadium been stuffed with and what's the fuss about

Workers at Cleveland Bridge, who built the Wembley Arch, claim to have put Middlesbrough memorabilia inside it. Fans now believe the ground is cursed.

which cartoon creatures is usain bolt faster than

At 23.35mph, Usain Bolt is faster than Roadrunner, who reached a top speed of 15mph, and Speedy Gonzales at 8mph. He's easily beaten by Sonic The Hedgehog, at 760mph.

what footballer scored a hat trick for his country but never scored for his club

Geoff Hurst scored a hat-trick for his country but never scored for his club. He played one county cricket game for Essex but scored no runs.

where was the 1st ever test match in cricket

The first ever officially recognised test match was between England and Australia on 15 March 1877 in Melbourne. The Australians won by 45 runs.

chick lit and trash tv

Real life is in HD all the time, but it'd sometimes seem drab without the added sparkle of Hollywood, Bollywood, Nollywood, our gossipy tabloids and, of course, the box of retina-pleasing delights which is the telly. Turn on and tune in to these answers-on-demand, repeated here and not, for once, on Dave. Or you could put this down and go and watch the whole of YouTube (for 1,754 years – not recommended).

? which actor coined the phrase elementary dear watson

Actor Clive Brook coined the phrase 'Elementary, my dear Watson' in the 1929 film *The Return of Sherlock Holmes*. The phrase wasn't in any of the original stories.

? how many characters have appeared in the simpsons

There are 149 recurring characters in *The Simpsons*, plus 237 featured characters who have appeared in one episode each. The stars get $400,000 an episode.

? did borat improve kazakstan tourism

The film *Borat* boosted tourism in Kazakhstan by 300%. Air Astana, the national carrier, even added a third weekly flight from Heathrow to its charter.

? roughly how many households owned television sets in britain at the end of the 60s, 70s, 80s and 90s – each decade please

In 1959, 16.1m homes had a TV. In 1969 it was 18.3m, 1979 was 20.2m, 1989 was 21.7m and 1999 was 24.7m. 88% of people's main TVs are now digital.

? what 4 films does spielberg watch before starting a new project

Before directing a movie, Steven Spielberg always looks at four films: *Seven Samurai*, *Lawrence of Arabia*, *It's a Wonderful Life* and *The Searchers*.

? is arnie in terminator one

O. J. Simpson was the original choice, but he was deemed too nice for it, so Arnold Schwarzenegger played the murderous robot in *The Terminator* (1984).

? **wot does darth vadar mean**

Fadir (pronounced 'fay-der') is Anglo-Saxon for father. Darth is invented – a variant of dark. Thus, Darth Vader implies, fittingly, dark father.

? **how are the newspapers distributed across the uk for the morning – it seems an incredible task to get to every shop, even ones in the middle of nowhere, every day, x**

Newspapers are printed and sent to the UK's three main distributors (Smiths, Menzies and Dawson), who have 124 depots. They then deliver to 54,000 retailers.

? **when was the first time batman and superman teamed up in the comics**

Batman and Superman first met in 'The Mightiest Team In The World' (*Superman* 76) in June 1952. They were on a cruise ship when a jewel thief struck.

? in the film valkyrie, bill nighy's character signs the order to deploy the home army in blue pencil: why blue

> Blue pencils are used in signing documents as they will not show up in lithographs, and therefore prevent duplication. Copy-editors also use blue pencils.

? at auction in 1976 doctor who's scarf was sold for how much

> Doctor Who's original scarf fetched £6,500 at a 1976 auction. The only official Doctor Who scarf hit the shops the same year, in 6ft and 10ft versions.

? where did the term flip the bird come from... as in to stick one's middle finger up

> In 19th century theatre, giving someone the bird meant hissing them, like a goose, as a means of disapproval. The Roman finger gesture took the name.

who did the voice for elma fudd

> Elmer Fudd: Arthur Q. Bryan (1940–59), Hal Smith (1960–1), Mel Blanc (1972–89), Jeff Bergman (1990–3) Greg Burson (1990–5) and Billy West (1996–present).

has there ever been a paper on xmas day

> Newspapers used to be published on Christmas Day. In 1912, 50 leading papers agreed to observe the holiday, but *The Times* did send copies to subscribers.

was shock rocker marilyn manson kevin's geeky sidekick on tv's the wonder years

> Marilyn Manson was not in *The Wonder Years*. There was a rumour that he played Kevin Arnold's friend Paul. Paul was actually played by Josh Saviano.

? in which film was a toilet first seen flushing

The first film to show a toilet flushing was Alfred Hitchcock's *Psycho*, in 1960. Hitch used chocolate syrup for blood in the infamous shower scene.

? in tragedy what is meant by hamarth

Hamartia is Aristotle's term for a tragic hero's fatal flaw. Othello's jealousy and Oedipus's hubris (pride) are examples from famous tragedies.

? how long approx. would it take to watch all the videos on youtube

It would take 15,379,200 hours, or 1,754 years, to watch all the videos on YouTube. Every minute, 10 hours of video are uploaded.

what is longest book in the world

The Yongle Dadian is the longest book ever written: an encyclopaedia of 11,095 volumes. It was written by 3,000 scholars over four years, from 1403.

where does james bond get his suits from

James Bond gets his suits from Tom Ford International. It is a recent change from the Brioni (Italian) suits he wore from 1995 to *Casino Royale* (2006).

what fictitious characters have won mtv lifetime achievement awards

Jason Voorhees (1992), Godzilla (1996) and Chewbacca (1997) won the MTV Lifetime Achievement Award. It became the MTV Generation Award in 2005.

? which tv reporter was reported dead in korean war but lived 2 tell tale

> Journalist Alan Whicker was erroneously reported dead whilst reporting on the Korean War. The newspaper obituary commented on his lack of achievement.

? what did pavarotti do for skate boarding

> Nothing. Humphrey Lyttelton introduced *I'm Sorry I Haven't A Clue* as 'the programme that does for comedy what Luciano Pavarotti does for skateboarding'.

? is quantum of solace the first ever james bond film where bond does not say, when asked his name, 'bond, james bond'

> *Quantum of Solace* is the fourth Bond film where Bond does not say 'Bond, James Bond'. The others: *From Russia With Love*, *Thunderball* and *You Only Live Twice*.

? **what was the pick up line side show bob used on edna krabapple in simpsons**

> Sideshow Bob woos Edna Krabappel with: 'I did once try to kill the world's greatest lover, but then I realised that there were laws against suicide.'

? **what was the first advert on channel 5**

> The first advert shown on Channel 5 was for Chanel No.5, Marilyn Monroe's favourite fragrance, in 1997. The channel rebranded itself as 'Five' in 2002.

? **how many dollars was the 1st tv set sold for**

> The first mass-produced mechanical TV set sold for $150 in 1928, which is $1,800.52 in today's money. It advertised cartoon drawings and dancing girls.

? what's the lowest score anyone's ever got on mastermind and what was their specialist subject

The lowest non-celebrity score on *Mastermind* was 7, by Colin Kidd. His specialist subject was World Chess Championships. The lowest celebrity score is 6.

? what is the shortest film in the world, and how long is it

The world's shortest film is *A Fassbinder Lie* by Turkish director Sabri Kalic. It is just 1/24 second (1 frame long), and has no interval.

? in the early days of batman, he used to shoot people with a gun – when did he stop using firearms

Batman stopped using a gun in 1940, after editor Whitney Ellsworth complained about Batman shooting some mutated men. Batman first appeared in 1939.

did max bygraves own the rights to the musical oliver

Yes. Max Bygraves bought the musical rights to *Oliver!* from writer Lionel Bart after 12 production companies rejected it in 1960. It was an instant hit.

which bond film was produced soonest after the respective novel and which film is said to most closely resemble the novel

You Only Live Twice was written in 1964 and filmed in 1967, the shortest gap from Bond novel to film. *On Her Majesty's Secret Service* is truest to the book.

how much money has jk rowling made per word

J. K. Rowling has made £526.54 per word written in the Harry Potter books. She's worth £576m in total and is the world's biggest selling living author.

how much is a copy of detective comics #27, may 1939

Detective Comics #27 can fetch up to £245,000. It features the first appearance of Batman and is the second most valuable comic after Action Comics #1.

what prop from a tv series caused a security alert

A prop from *Spooks* delayed London trains for an hour after a member of the public saw an 'oil drum' with wires sticking out of it at Deptford station.

what is hammocking in media

'Hammocking' is scheduling a less popular TV show between two more popular ones, hoping viewers watch it. Hammock is from the Haitian word for fish nets.

? what breed of cat does mrs mcclusky own

Mrs McCluskey's cat in *Desperate Housewives* is a solid blue British shorthair called Toby. Shorthairs are easy to train, making them suitable for TV.

? what's the world's most watched show

Strictly Come Dancing is the world's most-watched show. The BBC TV show has been replicated in 38 countries, including Chile and Japan.

? how many times is the word 'love' or its offsets, eg loving, lover etc, mentioned in 'moulin rouge' – we are watching it and drinking every time it's mentioned

The words 'love', 'loving', 'loved' and 'lover' occur in *Moulin Rouge* 146 times in total during its 2h 7m length. Expect to be very drunk by the end.

the animal
kingdom

Occupying a space in the universe approximately
between the Dalai Lama and parsley, the animal
kingdom is a bottomless source of wonderment.
Our furry/scaly/compound-eyed cousins can be cute,
mind-blowingly well designed, and quite often a bit
yucky. They obligingly produce a lot of facts, though.
It's worth knowing that if you've got a spare £140k
lying around, you could buy a pair of white lion cubs,
or enough bees to lift a person.

has there ever been an asbo imposed on an animal

Five-year-old cat Lewis was given an ASBO after savaging several people, including an Avon lady. It was allowed out only if its owner gave it Prozac.

if a 1 humped dromedary camel mated with the 2 humped bactrian camel then how many humps will the offspring be born with

Crossbreeding of dromedary and Bactrian camels produces larger, stronger offspring with a single, elongated hump. In Kazakhstan, they are called bukhts.

why are bird watchers called twitchers

'Twitcher' comes from the nervous tics of Howard Medhurst, a 1950s birdwatcher. Properly, only birders who 'tick off' species on a list are twitchers.

what was posted 450 miles by its german owner after it crawled into a parcel box for a nap

A cat was posted 450 miles by mistake after he crawled into a parcel box for a cat nap. He was owned by Gitti Rauch and travelled from Rottach to Dorsten.

could bees lift a man

Yes – a bumblebee weighs 0.052g. It can carry ¾ of its weight when collecting pollen and nectar. It would take 1,953,923 bumblebees to lift a man.

what animal has lived the longest

The longest-living animal yet found was a clam, found off Iceland's coast, which was found to have reached 405. It had to be killed to discover its age.

? how many vampire bats would it take to drain an average human of blood

It would take 500 vampire bats to drain the average human of blood. A vampire bat consumes an average of 10ml per feed. The body contains 5l (5000ml).

? so if you gave a cow helium, would its moos be high pitched like a human's voice goes when given helium or would it just stand on you

A cow's moo would be higher on helium, as sound travels faster in any air/helium mixture. It would still have a hissy fit and stand on you, though.

? wot animal can lick its own eyeball

The okapi, a deer-like mammal native to central Africa, can lick its own eyeballs and inside its ears with a 14in tongue. Its legs are stripy, like a zebra.

? can you get milk from pigeons

Pigeons produce crop milk – a thick liquid which contains more protein and fat than cow or human milk. The crop is located under the throat.

? how heavy is a blue whale

Blue whales have an average mass of 143 tonnes and can grow up to 30m long. This gives a BMI of 159, which is quite seriously obese.

? how high can a butterfly

Glider pilots have seen monarch butterflies flying as high as 11,000ft. They're capable of transatlantic flight and have been spotted in SW Britain.

? what did frodo baggins have to do with the monster ravin loony party

In February 2000, Frodo Baggins was the first pet (a dog) to enter Britain with a passport – an idea originally suggested by the Monster Raving Loony Party.

how long is an ant-eater's tongue

A giant anteater's tongue is 60cm long and can be flicked in and out of the mouth 150 times a minute. From nose to tail, the giant anteater is 2.1m long.

how much is a honey bee worth

A honey bee costs 7p. A frame of 450 individuals (including a queen) costs £30. Bees need to visit 2 million flowers to create 1lb of honey.

has there ever been a reported story of badgers stopping humans leaving their home

In 2003, a belligerent badger trapped the Youngs family from Worcestershire inside their house for two hours. An expert used jam sandwiches to catch it.

? every year how many lambs does one sheep have

Most breeds of sheep produce single or twin lambs. Ewes have 17-day oestrus cycles. Freemartins are ewes without ovaries. 8% of rams are gay.

? what can't walk backwards

Any walking creature can move backwards to some degree, but kangaroos can't walk backwards firmly. It's a myth that cows and emus can't walk backwards.

? how loud is a dolphin's squeak

Dolphin vocalisations have been clocked at 228 decibels. This is louder than a jet engine (120 decibels) and even an air raid siren (150 decibels).

? who's the largest elephant in europe

The Netherlands' Emmen zoo's Radza is now the largest bull elephant in Europe. He was born in 1966 in Mysore, India. He is 3.15m tall, and weighs 7200kg.

❓ what breed is grommit the dog

Gromit of Wallace & Gromit is a beagle. He reads *The Daily Beagle*, went to Dogwarts University and likes knitting and cooking. His birthday is on 12 February.

❓ how many litres of milk does a baby humpback whale suck from its mother per day

Humpback whale calves drink 240 litres of milk per day. Imagine 423 pints on your doorstep. The fat content gives it the consistency of cottage cheese.

❓ what has a record of 10.6 miles per hour

10.6mph is the land speed record for a crocodile, set by a galloping Australian freshwater crocodile. Most croc species 'belly run' rather than gallop.

? what's the heaviest gorilla ever recorded

> N'gagi, the world's heaviest gorilla, weighed in at a whopping 310kg. He was 1.72m tall with a chest of 198cm. He died aged 18 in San Diego Zoo in 1944.

? what is the name of the tropical bird that builds their nest upside down and how come the chicks don't fall out

> Swiftlets build their nests upside down from saliva and blood mixed with leaves. The eggs are glued in with saliva. They are constructed in caves in Asia.

? approximately how big is the brain of an average domestic cat

> The brain of a typical domesticated cat is 5cm long and weighs 30g. A human brain is 15cm long and weighs 1,400g. Women's are slightly smaller than men's.

? can owls turn their heads 360 degrees

Owls can't turn their heads in a 360-degree circle, but can turn them 135 degrees in each direction. They need this ability, as they can't move their eyes.

? which animal reproduces a million in 18 months

Rats multiply so quickly that in 18 months a pair of rats could have over a million descendants. They can reach sexual maturity at five weeks of age.

? what is the highest ranking animal in the armed forces

Simon, ship's cat of the HMS *Amethyst*, received the honorary rank of Able Seacat, as well as three medals, for continuing to serve despite shrapnel wounds.

how long can a cockroach survive after its head has been cut off

A cockroach could live for a month without its head. Their brains do not control their breathing, and they can survive without food for a month.

tell me about the tallest penguin

The emperor penguin is the tallest, at 1.2m. It would take 320,335,834 on top of each other to reach the moon. Penguin meat has a fishy taste.

how many rattlesnakes would you need to fill a pint glass with venom

You'd need 668 rattlesnakes to produce a pint of venom. When 'milked', they would each yield an average of 0.85ml. As much as 3.9ml has been recorded.

? **in financial terms which is the most expensive animal inna world**

> The South African white lion is the most expensive animal in the world. A white lion cub costs about £70,000 to buy and is considered a divine creature.

? **wots the most poisonous spider in australia**

> The Sydney funnel-web spider is the most poisonous spider in Australia. It can grow up to 3in across, and an untreated bite can kill in less than an hour.

? **what is the longest animal in the world**

> The worm Lineus longissimus (no common name) is the world's longest animal. A scarily long 55m (180ft) specimen was washed ashore on a beach in Scotland in 1864.

do bumblebees have bones

No, bumblebees have skeletons, but no bones. Their skeletons are on the outside (exoskeletons) and are made of flexible chitin, not bone.

how many brains does a slug have

A slug has one brain. Slugs can learn: scientists trained slugs to avoid their favourite food, potatoes, by feeding them nasty-tasting potatoes.

is there such a thing as a fish that can eat monkeys

Yes, Asian arowana can jump several feet into overhanging branches to catch and eat small monkeys. In South America, arowanas are nicknamed water monkeys.

how many ears does a praying mantis have

The praying mantis has a single ear with two separate eardrums. In the form of a slit, it's situated in the chest and can hear frequencies above 20,000 hz.

do turkeys live in trees

Turkeys don't live in trees, but wild turkeys living in forests roost in trees overnight. Wild turkeys can fly at 55mph. Only male turkeys (toms) gobble.

did james bond step on real crocodiles in 'live and let die'

The crocodiles in *Live and Let Die* were real. The directors had a pond constructed on a Jamaican crocodile farm. The scene took 5 takes to get right.

how many registered pigeon flyers are in the united kingdom

Although racing is declining by 5% a year, there remain 37,000 pigeon racers in 2,500 pigeon clubs in the UK. A pigeon belonging to the Queen won a race in 1990.

planet earth

Waking up every day here on Earth doesn't surprise us (at least, not most mornings), but there are tons of surprising things about it once you've got out of bed and put your socks on. AQA 63336 would love to have been a Geography teacher, telling eager classes about Licking the Birse and Hitler's fondness for Blackpool, but the bulky tweed jacket means, sadly, it wouldn't fit inside today's mobile phones.

? which port town has the
nickname monkey killers
after hanging a monkey
mistakenly thinking it was
a french sailor

> Allegedly, during the Napoleonic war,
> the people of Hartlepool hanged a
> monkey, believing it was a French spy.
> They are now known as monkey
> hangers.

? in which village did a vicar
marry a pig, christen a lamb
and bury a hog all in the
same week

> Gainford, County Durham, is the
> village where the vicar of St Mary's
> Church married a Pigg, christened a
> Lamb and buried a Hogg all in the
> same week.

? what city in england does
not have any roads

> The City of London doesn't have any
> roads. There are streets, alleys and
> lanes, but no roads. It's a separate
> city of one square mile within greater
> London.

? **what are the top 5 cities for traffic congestion in europe and where does bristol rank**

> Europe's most congested cities:
> London (11.8mph), Berlin (15mph),
> Warsaw (16.1mph), Manchester
> (17.4mph), Edinburgh (18.5mph).
> Bristol is 8th (19.6mph).

? **how long did it take the hoover dam to fill with water**

> The Hoover Dam was completed in
> 1935 and it took until July 1941 for
> water to fill Lake Mead, the reservoir
> created by the dam. At the bottom of
> the lake is a B-29 Superfortress
> bomber.

? **capital of the world**

> The United Nations HQ in New York
> City is the best candidate for world
> capital. It's on international territory,
> has 192 member states and aims for
> world peace.

**? what were the dates of the
2 previous attempts to
make the channel tunnel
and how far did the
victorians dig**

In 1881, the English dug 1,893m and
the French 1,669m in the first
attempt at a Channel Tunnel
(eventually opened in 1994). In 1974,
construction work began briefly
again.

**? when did people start
celebrating new year**

The New Year holiday was first
celebrated in Babylon 4,000 years
ago, on the first day of spring. In
153 BC, Rome declared 1 January as
the New Year.

**? where is the most inland
point on the surface of the
earth**

The furthest point from the sea is the
Eurasian pole of inaccessibility. It's in
the Dzoosotoyn Elisen desert in China
and is 1,645 miles from the sea.

when was newcastle upon tyne's third largest export urine

Newcastle exported human urine for use in textile dyeing during the 17th century. The urine was collected from public urinals or barrels in the city.

whereabouts is the nearest desert to sittingbourne

At 599.4 miles, the Bardenas Reales, a small desert in Navarra, Spain, is the closest to Sittingbourne, Kent. Europe's largest desert is in Iceland.

how many rain drops in the sea

There are 4 septillion (4, then 24 zeros) raindrops in the sea. 137 quintillion (137, then 18 zeros) litres of water fill the Earth's oceans.

where is the highest village in britain

Flash, Staffordshire, is the highest village in Britain, 463m above sea level. The Cairnwell Pass on the A93 is the highest main road, at 670m.

? what ghost haunts the french house in soho

Francis Bacon (d.1992) is said to haunt the French House pub in Soho. The figurative painter, known for his grotesque style, drank and gambled there.

? did people who committed suicide used to get staked through the heart

From medieval times till 1823 (when an Act of Parliament prevented the practice), suicides were staked through the heart and buried at public crossroads.

? where did hitler want to base himself in england if they won the war

Hitler planned to base himself in Blackpool if Germany won the war, and spared it from the Blitz. He wanted to unfurl the Nazi flag from Blackpool Tower.

? **if earth was the size of a grain of salt, how big would our universe be**

> If Earth was the size of a grain of salt, the universe would be 12.9 trillion miles wide, the Milky Way 14 million miles, and the solar system 600ft.

? **why are the streets of caracas blocked off on xmas eve**

> In Caracas, the capital of Venezuela, it is customary for the streets to be closed off on Christmas Eve so that people can roller-skate to church.

? **is my girlfriend wanting a lazy day or is it really unlucky to do any cleaning on new year's day**

> In China, it's considered unlucky to clean on New Year's Day because it sweeps away the year's good fortune. Your girlfriend doesn't want to chance it.

? parachutes were dropped on the city of st louis, usa, in the 1930s to commemorate which event

In February 1930, milk was parachuted from a plane over St Louis to commemorate the first flight by a cow in an aeroplane. The cow was milked on the flight.

? where in the world do people ride a massive tree trunk downhill – they hold on to chains attached to the tree and people die doing it

In the Suwa area of Nagano, the Onbashira festival includes the kiotoshi ceremony, where people slide 100m down 39-degree slopes on 12-ton tree trunks.

? what's under the ladybyer reservoir

Ladybower reservoir in Derbyshire was built over the villages of Derwent and Ashopton. It was built between 1935 and 1943, and took two further years to fill.

where does the word alcatraz come from

Alcatraz's name is from Juan Manuel de Ayala, who named it Isla de los Alcatraces (isle of gannets). It can also mean pelicans. He really saw cormorants.

what was the name of the village in france where in 1515 everyone danced for a month

The Dancing Plague of July 1518 occurred in Strasbourg, France. Over the month that they danced, most people died of heart attack, stroke or exhaustion.

how long ago did the first class-based societies develop

The earliest class-based society was in the Zhou Dynasty, China (1046–256 BC). The 'Four Occupations' rankings were (high to low) shi, gong, nong and shang.

? at what point of cornwall does the english channel end and atlantic start

The English Channel becomes the Atlantic at the line between Land's End in Cornwall and Ushant off Brittany. The Channel covers an area of 29,000 sq miles.

? when were gnomes brought over to this country

The first garden gnomes came into the UK in 1847. A set of 21 was imported from Germany by Sir Charles Isham, for his garden at Lamport Hall, Northants.

? what is the coldest recorded temperature in celsius in england

The lowest temperature recorded in England was –26.1°C on 10 January 1982 at Edgmond, near Newport, in Shropshire. The highest was 38.5°C in Kent in 2003.

how long does morning last on the moon

The Moon has a day and a night, but each is nearly two weeks long. Assuming half the daylight hours are morning, morning lasts for almost 328 hours.

my french wife is expecting twins (i am british), if she gave birth on an american submarine under the north pole, what nationality would the twins be

You'd be in international waters, so the twins would inherit the parents' nationality: dual British and French. Nearest baby formula: Longyearbyen, Spitsbergen (800 miles).

what is the most abundant coin in the world

The most abundant coin in the world is the US 1 cent coin. Over 300 billion have been minted since 1787, and around 200 billion are still in circulation.

? who used propaganda using superman saving children from land mines

The US Government and UNICEF joined with DC Comics in 1996 to produce 'Superman: Deadly Legacy'. The comic aimed to help promote landmine awareness.

? what's the first country to celebrate new year's day

Tonga is the first country to celebrate New Year's Day. Samoa, only 600 miles away but on the other side of the international dateline, is last.

? which town in england had the first crematorium

Woking was the first town in England to have a crematorium. Building work started in 1878, and the first cremation in Britain took place there on 26 March 1886.

? i am having a drunken conversation with my friend jon; i claim that on a clear day you can see scotland from the top of mount snowdon – i'm correct aren't i

> Yes. The view between Snowdon and Merrick (southern Scotland) is the longest line of sight in the British Isles, at 144 miles (232km) on a very clear day.

? what country has the longest name

> Libya's local name is Al Jumahiriyah al Arabiyah al Libiyah ash Shabiyah al Ishtirakiyah al Uzma, making it the longest country name in the world.

? what is the smallest county in the uk

> Rutland is the smallest county in the UK. The Isle of Wight is actually smaller at high tide, but official measurements are taken at low tide.

what is the average life expectancy of a cloud

Cumulus clouds have an average life of 64 minutes, cumulonimbus 124 and nimbostratus 145. A cloud droplet is 1,000 times smaller than a raindrop.

is there undeniable proof of how old the world is

Yes. The Earth's age of 4.54 billion years has been determined by radiometric age dating of meteorite samples. Humans have been around for 0.01% of the Earth's life.

everything in numbers

Some are very, very big, and some are very, very small. Love them or hate them, without them you couldn't catch a bus, buy bananas, arrange a hot date, or send a text. Putting different numbers together can add up to some very useful information indeed: for example, for every giraffe in the world, 20 pairs of clogs are made each year in Holland. See? More usable than a quadratic equation.

? what percent of united states population insure themselves against alien abduction

0.01% of the US population is insured against alien abduction. Policy payouts vary from $10,000 to $10 million. One company has paid out on two cases.

? how many brain cells would fit in a grain of sand

1 million brain cells fit in a grain of sand. If your cells were the size of sand, you'd be 180m tall. There are 7 quadrillion atoms in a cell.

? how many pubs in london, england and the uk are named after dukes or duchesses

1,990 pubs in London, 6,985 in England and 7,150 in the UK are named after dukes or duchesses. The most popular is the Duke of York (4,329 in the UK).

how many people have been hanged in england since records began

10,902 hangings have taken place in England since records began, with 10,378 of them being men. As well as hangings, 32 women were burned at the stake.

how many labrador dog hairs would it take to fill a duvet cover

There are approx 6,000 hairs/sq in on a labrador, hence 1,400/cub in. A duvet cover is 18,500 cubic inches – 27,750,000 labrador hairs fit in a duvet.

how many ipods are sold each year and each second

10.2 million iPods are currently sold worldwide every year. This equates to 0.32 every second. The UK market accounts for 17% of the total.

how many led screens were used in eurovision 2009

Moscow used 30% of the world's entire stock of LED screens on their lavish Eurovision stage in 2009. Over £30 million was spent on the contest.

what does 10004180204 mean

10004180204 is written by diners leaving a restaurant to explain why they haven't paid, as it can read 'One owes nothing for one ate nothing to owe for.'

wot is the largest charity in the world

The biggest charity in the world is the Stichting INGKA Foundation, with $36 billion. It was set up to promote architecture and design, and owns Ikea.

? how many cars are produced in the world each day

142,144 cars are produced each day worldwide, an annual output of 51m. At current population growth rates, 2.68 babies are born for each new car.

? how many ping pong balls would it take to refloat the titanic

It would take 1,354,432,405 pingpong balls (33.5 cu cm, 2.7g) to float the *Titanic* (41,730,498,040g). The calculation is: *Titanic* weight/(ball volume – ball weight).

? ok, what's the most 1st time winners in any one formula one season

1982 had the most maiden victories in F1. Patrick Tambay, Michele Alboreto, Riccardo Patrese, Elio de Angelis and Keke Rosberg all won for the first time.

? who produces the largest amount of tyres in the world

Lego produces the largest number of tyres in the world – over 300 million annually. About 19 billion separate Lego elements are produced every year.

? what much loved tv character did over 2.5 thousand people try to call after his number appeared on his show

2,500 people tried to call the Doctor during the Doctor Who episode 'The Stolen Earth'. His number (07700900461) is a fake number reserved for TV dramas.

? how many mammals have had homosexual experiences

228 species of mammal have had documented homosexual experiences, as have 146 species of bird. Giraffes engage in more same-sex than opposite-sex acts.

? how many clogs are produced in holland per year to nearest half million

> 3 million pairs of clogs are made in Holland each year. The UK's last clog maker is Walkley Clogs; they make specialist clogs and even export to Holland.

? if you were to add up all the presents in 12 days of christmas how many would you receive

> 364 presents are given by 'my true love' throughout the 'Twelve Days of Christmas': 184 birds, 140 performing (or milking) people, and 40 golden rings.

? how many coffees are drunk in london each day

> 5.5m cups of coffee are drunk every day in London, compared to 4m pints of beer. The most expensive coffee in the world costs £365 per kg.

? **does everyone have a phone**

> 57.8% of the world's population have never received a telephone call. Furthermore, 75.3% of the world's population has never accessed the internet.

? **how many people graduate from chinese universities each year**

> 6 million students will graduate from Chinese universities this year. These will join the 1.5 million graduates from last year who have yet to find jobs.

? **if every penny was picked up off the floor in england how much money would it amount to**

> 6.5bn 1p coins are missing, making £65m. £26m is on the streets, £11m in handbags, £7.8m in cars and £5.9m in sofas. They weigh 23,140 tonnes.

? on average how many computer viruses are released per month

600 new viruses are released to the internet each month. 80,000 viruses now exist. In January 2003, the Slammer virus infected 75,000 computers in 10 minutes.

? why does february only have 28 days rather than the normal 30/31?

Roman king Numa Pompilius, who invented January and February, felt the latter to be an unlucky, dreary, wintry month, so gave it just 28 days.

? why is 999 the emergency number

999 was chosen as the emergency number because it was easy to convert public telephone boxes to make calls free of charge if they included the number 9.

? what is the biggest irish peopled city in the world

Boston has the highest Irish population of any non-Irish city in the world, at 96,225. Dublin has a population of 1.1 million; 840,000 are Irish.

? which small country had the highest toilet queue in europe

Brussels set the record for the world's longest toilet queue in March 2009. 756 people crossed their legs in line to raise awareness for World Water Day.

? what is the oldest cheese in england

Cheshire is the oldest English cheese. It's mentioned in the Domesday Book, but is thought to have been made in Chester in Roman times or earlier.

? approximately how many flowers does it take for one bee to make 1lb of honey

Nectar from 2m flowers is needed to make 1lb of honey. Bees collect it in their special honey stomachs, visiting up to 1,500 flowers for just 70mg.

? what is the biggest snowman ever made

The biggest snowman was built by the people of Bethel in Maine, USA, in 2008. It was 122ft 1in tall and weighed 13,000,000lb. The eyes were 5ft wreaths.

? which country has the most plastic surgery

Switzerland has the most plastic surgery procedures per capita, at 2.15 per 1,000 people. Cyprus is 2nd at 1.86 and the UK is 28th at 0.08 per 1,000.

who wore the first pair of roller skates

The first pair of roller skates was worn by a Belgian musical instrument maker who rolled into a party in London while playing the violin on 22 April 1760.

what is the highest price paid for a piece of football memorabilia

The oldest surviving FA Cup (from 1896) was auctioned for £478,000 in 2005, making it the most expensive item of football memorabilia.

what's the highest recorded sand castle

On 31 May 2007, a record 49.55ft high sandcastle was built at Myrtle Beach, southern California. Tropical storm Barry knocked 6ft off it four days later.

what is the world record for throwing a washing machine

Discus thrower Dariusz Slowik from Poland holds the record for throwing a washing machine. He launched a 48kg one an incredible 3.5 metres in November 2008.

how many people have been in outer space

Up to November 2008 there have been 489 people, from 38 countries, who have flown in space. Space is defined as anywhere above the Karman Line, 62.1 miles up.

where are the biggest visible letters in the uk

The biggest visible letters in the UK are on the Oxo Tower (3m each). Next are 'In These Stones Horizons Sing' (2m) at Cardiff's Wales Millennium Centre.

? what years have we had really bad winters in the uk

The coldest UK winter on record was in 1684, when coaches travelled along the frozen River Thames. The winter of 1962–3 was the coldest since 1740.

? what is the closest any human being has been to the centre of the earth

The crew of the bathyscaphe *Trieste* dived to a depth of 6.77 miles in the Pacific Ocean in 1960. This put them 3,952 miles from the centre of the Earth.

? what got into itself after 19 years of trying in 1974

The *Guinness Book of World Records* entered itself as the best-selling copyrighted book of all time in 1974, 19 years after it was launched in 1955.

where is the highest telephone box in the world

The highest payphone in the world is found on Sears Tower Skydeck observation platform in Chicago, 1,353ft (412m) above ground.

who has the biggest collection of spoons on the planet

The largest collection of spoons belongs to Australian Des Warren, who has 35,000. The Passaic County Historical Society (New Jersey) exhibits 5,400.

what was the longest note held in a top 40 hit

The longest note held in a UK hit lasts 20.2 seconds, by Morten Harket of A-Ha, in 'Summer Moved On'. It got to No. 33 in 2000. Bill Withers reached 18sec in 'Lovely Day'.

what's the biggest sausage

The longest sausage ever made was 36.75 miles long. It was assembled by J. & J. Tranfield in South Yorkshire in 2000. The largest hotdog was 104.75ft long.

where in uk has there been the most lotto winners

The luckiest UK places for Lotto winners are the Medway towns in Kent. They have one winner for every 6,119 people in the area. Ilford is close behind.

which living person's autograph is currently the most valuable in the world

The most valuable signature of any living person, at £16,545, is that of Neil Armstrong. William Shakespeare's is the most valuable in the world, at £3m.

what regiment has the most vc in the british army

The Royal Green Jackets have been awarded more Victoria Crosses than any other unit, with a total of 56. Their motto is *celer et audax* ('swift and bold').

what is the world record for staying under water

The world record for the longest time underwater without taking a breath is an incredible 21min 29sec, held by Hungarian David Merlini since 26 April 2009.

how many times did big ben 'bong' in the year 2000

Big Ben bonged 57,096 times in 2000 – 156 bongs on each of 366 days. The bong is an E. Londoners heard 35,136 of the tuneful ¼-hour chimes that year.

what's the biggest hamburger

The world's largest commercially available hamburger is 74.75kg (164.8lb). It is sold at Mallie's Sports Grill & Bar in Michigan, and costs £271.55.

do you know where the biggest christmas scene in the world is, please

The world's largest nativity scene is in Grignan, in Provence, France. Lise Berger has crafted a miniature 'nativity village' of over 1,000 figures.

wot is the world's tallest manmade viewing platform

The world's tallest man-made viewing platform is the Grand Canyon Skywalk. At 4,000ft, it exceeds those of the world's largest skyscrapers.

a study of language

Things can be difficult without words. Pointing can only get you so far, and it's certainly not ideal as an attempt to chat someone up. Faced with this problem some years ago, Homo sapiens had to stop grunting and shrieking and start taking evening classes in Italian. AQA 63336 answers are all in English (which is officially the best language, due to its hilarious spelling), but still covers the marvellous range of ways we communicate, from Tarzan's yell to Presidential speeches.

? could you text the bible to someone

There are 4,017,010 characters in the Bible. A text message is limited to 160 characters, so 25,107 messages would be needed to text the whole Bible.

? when was 'raining cats and dogs' first used

The first verified use of 'raining cats and dogs' was in 1738 by Jonathan Swift. In Northern European myths, the cat stood for rain and the dog for wind.

? what does wd40 stand for

WD-40 stands for Water Displacement, 40th formula. Industrial chemist Norm Larsen developed the correct formula to prevent corrosion on his 40th attempt.

? what is the weirdest, most bizarre thing you could call someone

An ill-roasted egg is the most bizarre thing to call someone. Cream-faced loon and greasy, elf-skinned hypocrite are also good. All are from Shakespeare.

? when was the first emoticon used

The first emoticon appeared in the transcript of an 1862 speech by Abraham Lincoln, but some say it was a typo. :-) was created by Scott Fahlman in 1982.

? why is cannabis referred to as pot

The word 'pot', for cannabis, comes from the Mexican-Spanish word *potiguaya*, meaning marijuana leaves. It's been in use in English since the 1930s.

how many phobias are there in the world

There are an infinite number of phobias, but about 700 commonly recognised ones. Hippopotomonstrosesquipedaliophobia is the fear of long words.

what does the anglo saxon word 'wed' mean

The Anglo-Saxon word 'wed' or 'wedd' means to wager or gamble. In context, it's all about the groom's purchase of the bride from her father, for a fee.

where does posh come from

Posh dates back to at least 1867 in the sense of meaning a dandy or fop. It's from Romany gypsy language. It's a myth that it stands for 'port out, starboard home'.

? is there a word for words spelt in alphabetical order, for example the word abort

An abecedarian word is a word whose letters appear in alphabetical order. Around 0.03% of English words fulfil this property. 'Aegilops' is the longest.

? what is a dutchman, apart from a dutch man

A Dutchman is a strip of material used to cover the join between two pieces of theatre scenery. It's also a knot used to secure loads on trucks.

? wot do you call a book of spells

A grimoire is a book of spells. The earliest known is the Picatrix, originally written in Arabic in the 10th century, then translated into Spanish and Latin.

? what toy does an arctophile collect

An arctophile is a collector of teddy bears. It is derived from the Greek words 'arcto' (bear) and 'philos' (lover). A plangonologist collects dolls.

? what is the ancient greek word for a moral dilemma, typically used in aristotle's virtue ethics when there is a conflict of virtues

Aporia (Greek for 'impassable') was Aristotle's word for a moral dilemma. In English, it's a rhetorical device in speech-making: the feigning of doubt.

? who said, 'fail to prepare, prepare to fail'

Benjamin Franklin said, 'By failing to prepare, you are preparing to fail.' He also said 'Beer is living proof that God loves us and wants us to be happy.'

? where does the word gruelling come from

The word 'gruelling' comes from the 18th century slang phrase 'to get one's gruel', meaning to receive a punishment. It means punishing or exhausting.

? did the v sign come about from archers

The two-finger (V-sign) gesture represents the vagina. It originated in Ancient Greece. It's an urban myth that it comes from cutting off archers' fingers.

? wot is the shortest complete sentence in the english language please

'Be' and 'Go' are the shortest sentences in English (not 'I am'). 'Jesus wept' is the shortest in the Bible. A joke has it that 'I do' is the longest sentence.

? is cotton wool made from cotton

Cotton wool comes from raw cotton fibre. Dr Joseph Sampson Gamgee invented cotton wool in 1880. Samwise Gamgee from *Lord of the Rings* is named after him.

? how long have people been speaking for

Full language capacity had evolved by 100,000 BC. Sumerian and Egyptian were the first written languages, in 3200 BC. Chinese and Greek were written in 1500 BC.

? a name for a small junk

Names for smaller variants of junks (Chinese ships) are quarter, half, third, zaw and kakam. The biggest (9-masted) medieval Chinese junks held 1,000 men.

why does the spanish nativity scene have a urinating and defecating character in it

A caganer, or defecating man, in Catalan Nativity scenes is a symbol of good luck, fertility and humility. Modern caganers are often based on celebrities.

which languages have a different conception of time than english – please name languages that do not write left 2 right

Hopi (a Native American language) has no words, grammatical constructions or expressions relating to time. Arabic and Hebrew are written right to left.

what do you call a boomerang that doesn't come back

The kylie is a boomerang designed not to return. Aboriginal hunters use boomerangs to scare birds, and kylies to hit them out of trees.

❓ why is 1 sheep called sheep but 10 sheep are still called sheep

> Old English had 'scep' (one sheep) and 'sceap' (more than one), but the two words began to be pronounced more and more alike, until the distinction disappeared.

❓ of all the words in the english language, what word has the most definitions

> 'Set' has 464 definitions – the most of all the words in English. 'Run' has 396 definitions, 'go' 368, 'take' 343 and 'stand' 334. 'The' is the most commonly used.

❓ priest returns to poet begins with e and ends in t with 5 letters

> The answer is Eliot, as in the poet T. S. Eliot. Eli was a famous biblical priest, who trained Samuel, and then you add the word 'to' backwards.

❓ what is the chinese translation of coca cola

The Chinese for Coca-Cola is K'o K'ou K'o Le. The Mandarin characters approximate the sound of the name and mean 'to allow the mouth to experience joy'.

❓ what is the devil's note

The 'Devil's Note' is actually an interval, rather than a note: a tritone. The medieval Church banned its use in compositions, except to represent Satan.

❓ what is the longest palindrome in the english dictionary

The longest single palindromes in English are 'redivider' and the scientific 'detartrated'. 'Saippurakaruppias' (Finnish for soap seller) is the world's longest.

what is a poet laureate

The Poet Laureate is appointed to write poetry for royal occasions (birthdays, weddings, etc). The Laureate is paid £5,750 and 682 bottles of sherry a year.

where does the saying beaten hands down come from

The saying 'beaten hands down' comes from horse racing, referring to a jockey winning so easily that he relaxes his posture towards the race's end.

what's the lobster shift

The lobster shift is a slang term for the night shift in places like factories or newspapers. It comes from the hour lobstermen go out to fish.

what is the name of the comical awards thing with regards to people that have sued companies for pathetic reasons

> The Stella Awards are given to ridiculous lawsuits. They are named after Stella Liebeck, who was awarded $2.9 million after spilling coffee on herself.

can i have a consonant please, carol

> You certainly can, young scholar. Have a t, then a w,y,n,d,y,l,l,y,n,g and you'll have AQA's favourite obsolete all-consonant word: twyndyllyng (twin).

where does the term skull as a cheers type thing come from

> The term 'skull' as a toast comes from the Scandinavian word 'skal', meaning bowl. A drinking-bowl would be offered to guests, as an act of hospitality.

? how often does a friday 13th occur

There's at least one Friday the 13th in every year. Sometimes there are two, and every 28 years there are three, in January, April and July. This will happen in 2012.

? when i am forward i am tense when i am back i am sweet what am i

You are an accent. A forward-sloping accent is grave, which can mean tense, and it also marks a word's tense; backward-sloping is acute (cute/sweet).

? wot is a habub

A habub, or haboob, is a type of dust storm that blows in the deserts of North Africa and the Arabian Peninsula. Hubbub means loud noise and habib means loved.

you couldn't make it up

off-the-wall answers

It's not easy being brilliant. 19 out of 20 applicants to become an AQA researcher fall at the first fence, with only the finest thoroughbreds making it through to the lush, green paddocks of researcherdom. However, it has to be admitted that there's a rare skill and imagination needed to come up with some of the answers we see in our application tests. Some might say they come from an entirely different stable altogether. Read on with admiration as we showcase some of the most special answers from applicants who never got hired.

? how many london tube stations start with f

> Out of the 14 London tube stations available, none actually start with F. Driving may be the best option if wanting to see the letter F while commuting.

? how much does the 'mail on sunday' cost

> The cost of mail on Sundays is the same as any other day of the week, but since the post offices are not open then there is really no cost.

? a mouse has invaded my pantry – what's the best way to kill it humanely

> *Applicant A:* Humane mouse traps can be bought from pest control shops. Once caught, you can put it outside, or kill it by carefully snapping its neck with tweezers.
>
> *Applicant B:* A humane method is to hold the mouse by the tail, pin the neck firmly to a table with a screwdriver. Pull the tail quickly, breaking its neck.

? in percentage terms, how much bigger is 20 than 15

> Twenty is 5% more than fifteen.
> Think of it as five equals 5%, ten is
> 10%, and so on. It's the same even if
> you're dressed to the nines. Count on
> it.

? how do you meditate

> A mediator helps parties develop a
> shared understanding of the conflict
> and to work toward building a
> practical and lasting resolution.

? over how many years should i depreciate a computer

> Computers depreciate in value as soon
> as they are purchased. You should sell
> your computer as soon as possible
> before it depreciates further.

? how many mister men characters are there and which is the best

> Very interesting question? I will
> research and let you know.

? **where was prince philip born**

Prince Philip was born in Greece and Denmark at the Greek Royal residence of Mon Repos on the island of Corfu on 10 June 1921.

? **can you still lose weight if you get a takeaway once a week**

Takeaways have a lot of calories per meal. To lose weight if you are eating a takeaway once a week make sure you do not eat much else.

? **what would be a good starter if i'm doing boeuf bourguignon followed by pear tarte tatin**

When preparing to make boeuf bourguignon a good start would be to cut the beef up into 100gm cubes and then put them into a bowl to marinate.

? is kevin peterson a solid,
top flight cricketer or just
arrogant and unreliable
with a bat

> Everyone is entitled to their own
> opinion, however, many people will
> have different opinions and may not
> always agree.

? which elements have been
discovered since tom lehrer
sang about them

> Tom Lehrer, a professor at day and a
> satirist at night, composed a song
> containing all the elements. DeBuvitz
> found the element moron.

? who are fulham playing on
bocing day

> Bocing day is for the people who are
> gambling. If someone addicted to
> such things they will loose money and
> themselves.

? wot iz honny swarky mally ponce – i think it's french

Applicant A: It seems one would think so, but that sentence is not French for sure, it is English and it means 'darling kiss my pimp': Thank you.

Applicant B: Ponce is French for sandpaper. Perhaps this is a type of sandpaper used in the making of French furniture. Honey could refer to the colour of wood.

Applicant C: 'Honny swarky mally ponce' is a French phrase which translates as 'You have a fly on your nose.' Globally, there are over 130,000 species of fly.

? what fish should i order in the fish and chip shop – i don't want cod as it's being overfished

Cod worm is known to appear in cod, haddock, flounder, sole, halibu and to a lesser extend in swordfish and monkfish. Get anything else.

? **what is the area of a circle**
whose diameter is 10cm

> Can't answer. (I know the formula, but
> can't calculate it.)

? **how many paper planes laid**
end to end would reach from
london to pluto

> It would take 95 paper planes to reach
> from London to Pluto.

? **who regulates 63336**

> The Nuclear Regulatory Commission
> (NRC) has been regulating 63336
> since 1992 as part of the Energy
> Policy Act under President Bill
> Clinton.

surprising questions

It's always good to ask a silly question, because you're probably not the only one wondering; you're just the only one brave enough to ask. And it makes us laugh, so you'll be a hero twice over. No question is ever turned away for not passing its 11-plus; indeed, we love to extend the hand of edification to the neediest. Like these.

? can seagulls lay crocodiles

Seagulls cannot lay crocodiles. They lay eggs in clutches of 1–4 on cliff ledges. Incubation takes 28–30 days, when baby seagulls emerge.

? is a fox a dog or a cat

Foxes are in the same family (Canidae) as dogs, but are of a different genus (Vulpes for foxes, Canis for dogs). Cats are in the separate family Felidae.

? is guillemot a type of green avocado dip

Guacamole is a green avocado dip. A guillemot is a sea bird. You could try dipping tortilla chips in a guillemot, but it would probably peck you.

? what is the ship called in the film 'the mutiny on the bounty'

In *The Mutiny on the Bounty* the ship was called the *Bounty*. Master's Mate Fletcher Christian led 12 men in a mutiny on 28 April 1789.

? what type of animal is skippy the bush kangaroo

Skippy was the bush kangaroo, who lived in Australia. 'He' was actually female, and was an Eastern Grey kangaroo, Macropus giganteus.

? is a banana a fish

A banana is not a fish. A banana is naturally occurring, edible, nutritious, colourful, curvy and makes great cakes. This is in stark contrast to a fish. Hmm.

what swims faster: a 3-legged dog or a blind horse

A blind horse, guiding itself by scent alone at up to 30mph, swims faster than a three-legged dog. Three-legged dogs can swim, but not effectively or fast.

is belgium a country

Belgium is a country – a kingdom, in fact, where the Belgian people speak Flemish and French. It's also a customised-butter-figurine-making company.

how do you spell duck

D-u-c-k, unless you mean 'duct' as in duct tape. It was developed in 1942 for sealing WWII ammunition cases. It then became popular in households.

is orange a fruit

No, orange isn't a fruit but a colour. It's all in the indefinite article 'an', see: its presence for the fruit and its absence in the case of the colour.

are sheep cattle

No, sheep are ovine. They're more intelligent than cows, they have 32 teeth and horizontal slit-shaped pupils, and their average life expectancy is 10–12 years.

is london bigger than torquay

Using traditional 3D measuring techniques, London's bigger than Torquay. Torquay, first inhabited 37,000 years ago, is bigger in the fourth dimension of time.

what is a neandrofol is it a giant

A Neanderthal is an extinct human subspecies, with a flat, long skull and stocky frame. Neandrofols are as yet unknown, but may hail from Essex c.50,000 BC.

? what part of a pig does the truffle come from

Truffles are any of various fleshy, ascomycetous and edible fungi that grow underground and are valued as a delicacy. They are hunted for by pigs.

? where are a human's arms

Your arms are attached to your torso. The arm is made up of three main bones. Above your elbow you have the humerus, and below are the ulna and the radius.

? why japan called the land of the rising son

Japan is known as the 'Land of the Rising Sun' because the Japanese characters that make up Nippon ('Japan' in Japanese) mean sunrise.

? is there a dairy product on sale in the uk that is only available in france

No dairy products only available in France are on sale in the UK. The foulest-smelling French dairy thing is Morbier cheese, made from ash and leftovers.

? where is windsor castle

Windsor Castle is in Windsor, Berkshire. The castle is located in the Thames Valley, originally built by William the Conqueror to act as a defence for London.

? are prawns fish willies

Prawns are not fish willies. They are crustaceans or more commonly shellfish. They're sometimes called shrimp. A group of prawns is called a 'shoal'.

? why doesn't the sun set in north or south

The Earth rotates or spins toward the east. This is why the sun rises in the east and sets in the west, as do the moon, the planets and the stars.

? what's the opposite of a camel

The opposite of a camel is a soap dish. Quality examples (not the octopus sucker sort) have dips not humps, and most of their time is spent around water.

? will you marry me

AQA is honoured to be asked, but it would end in acrimony. You'd soon accuse AQA of infidelity as it continues to text millions of other people 24/7.

top 10 q&as

Our q&as range from the funny ha-ha to the funny-peculiar, with all flavours of funny in between. There are also some aspects of life which seem to trouble nearly everyone, and we often find ourselves soothing furrowed brows with answers to the same mysteries. Here are 2009's top 10 funniest, most bizarre, commonest and myth-bustingest.

the top 10 funniest

? is it ok to have sex with a dog

It is normal to be sexually attracted to a dog, but only if you are a dog yourself – in which case AQA is very impressed by your ability to use a mobile phone.

? how much does a ghost weigh

The average ghost weighs just 544g (1.2lb). Coincidentally, this is the exact same weight as the average white cotton bedsheet, minus two eyeholes.

? how can you test to see if someone is a god

You can test to see if someone is a god by saying 'It's a lovely day' to them. If they say 'Yes it is,' they're mortal. If they say 'Thanks,' bow down.

who is cleverer, a yorkshireman or a pigeon

A typical Yorkshireman has more brainpower than a pigeon. However, all pigeons have a good sense of direction, and some men never get out of Yorkshire.

are baboons evil

Yes, baboons are evil. Anything that steals your windscreen wipers while waving a red bum in your face is most definitely the work of the dark side.

how much does it cost to move a manhole

Moving a manhole (inc. local authority building regulation approval) costs a minimum of £600, plus £200 for a new cover. Moving a whole man costs a pint.

? who do i ask to help me
save the country, i'm
genuinely scared, brown
hasn't got a clue, please tell
me who to phone

> If you've got a problem, if no one else
> can help and if you can find them,
> maybe you can hire the A-Team.
> Otherwise you'll have to challenge
> Anneka Rice.

? can you tell me how to get
to the canteen on the death
star without being seen by
darth vader as i should be
on duty

> Avoid Vader by going past the
> hypermatter reactor control room.
> Then cut across the vent shafts. Do
> not use this route if under attack by
> rebel forces.

why did lady penelope never get laid by any of the thunderbirds

Lady Penelope clearly thought that there would be too many strings attached. Sleeping with the Thunderbirds can only lead to a complicated, tangled, mess.

if sam kar were a drink, what would she be

If Sam were a drink she would be a tequila slammer. She is fast, wild, unpredictable and usually causes a great deal of mischief.

the top 10 most bizarre

is the cartoon finding nemo based on a true story

Finding Nemo is not based on a true story. It's the story of a father's hunt for an errant clownfish and has grossed over £525 million worldwide.

? **i have just been eaten by a squirrel – how can i escape from its stomach**

Outstretch your arm and tickle the squirrel's soft palate. It will cough, then gag and vomit you up. You'll be a little damp but perfectly fine. Run away.

? **how many whole human bodies could you fit in 25 brunswick street sheffield, both whole or liquidised**

A house in Brunswick Street, Sheffield, could accommodate about 1,500 human bodies packed in very tightly, or about 1,800 in liquid form. Very messy.

? **how do you say in french i love you so much, you smell like sprouts**

'Je t'aime bien; tu as l'odeur des choux de Bruxelles' is French for 'I love you so much; you smell like sprouts'. AQA prefers a scent of vanilla.

? how fat do you have to be to stop a bullet

A 9mm round can penetrate 45cm of human flesh, so you'd need 45cm of fat to stop a bullet. As a bulletproof, average-height male, you'd weigh about 200kg.

? i am having trouble with my goldfish... can u suggest a cure to stop it talking

To cure a talking fish, put a large mirror at one end of the tank. Goldfish are quite shy and refuse to talk in the presence of a strange fish.

? we know the speed of light but what is the speed of dark

Darkness doesn't have a speed, as darkness is merely the absence of light. *The Speed of Dark* is a book by Elizabeth Moon, published by Orbit.

? how many bras would it take to displace the entire atlantic ocean

You would need 22,733,961 36C bras to displace the 323,600,000 cu km of water in the Atlantic Ocean (or a few dozen of Norma Stitz's 72ZZZ whoppers).

? how many otters can you fit in a watering can

The average size for a male otter is 40 inches long; a good size watering can is only around 30 inches. Common decency forbids forcing the otter inside.

? how many postage stamps would it take to cover the albert hall

It would take 34,645,569 regular-sized first class stamps to cover the walls, ceiling and floor of the Albert Hall. These stamps would be worth £13.5m.

the top 10 most asked

? who is the stig

Ben Collins is *Top Gear*'s Stig. He
appeared as himself when they played
car football and was named as a
'consultant' in Richard Hammond's
accident report.

? what's the meaning of life

Life has no meaning, it's just the
complex result of a sequence of
chemical reactions. Assign your own
meaning: find out what you love and
do it.

**? which came 1st, the chicken
or the egg**

The egg came first. DNA in the
fertilised egg of a chicken-like bird
mutated and that egg developed into
an embryo that emerged as the first
true chicken.

what are the 7 ancient wonders of the world

Seven ancient wonders: Pyramids, Babylon Hanging Gardens, Statue of Zeus, Temple of Artemis, Halicarnassus Mausoleum, Rhodes Colossus and Pharos of Alexandria.

why is the sky blue

Rayleigh scattering makes the sky blue. The blue part of sunlight has a short wavelength, so it hits air molecules, scatters off them, and you see it more.

why is it called boxing day

Boxing Day is so called as it was the traditional day for giving a tip ('Christmas box') to postmen, errand boys and staff. The term was coined in 1833.

why do men have nipples

Men's nipples develop before the gender of the embryo becomes male, as all embryos start off female. They have no real function except sexual pleasure.

how many countries are there in the world

There are 193 officially recognised countries in the world. Russia's the largest and Vatican City is the smallest. 53 list English as an official language.

how long is a piece of string

A piece of string is twice as long as half its length. It's usually shorter than the amount you need to wrap a parcel, but always long enough to tangle.

how does aqa work

AQA provides answers using intelligent algorithms, databases and human researchers. It's available 24/7 – even when you're abroad. See www.aqa.63336.com.

the top 10 myths

? do duck quacks have no echo

A duck's quack does echo. The urban myth that it does not may have arisen because ducks prefer open spaces over closed spaces, where echoes would occur.

? why do women have more ribs than men

Men and women both have 12 pairs of ribs (24 ribs in total). They protect the lungs and other internal organs. It is a myth that women have an extra rib.

? are polar bears right or left handed

It's a myth that polar bears are left-handed. They're ambidextrous (they use both hands equally well). Their fur is transparent and their skin is black.

how many spiders do you eat whilst sleeping in your lifetime

Most humans do not eat any spiders in their sleep. It was a myth started by journalist Lisa Holst to show how facts are believed and can be quickly spread by people.

how do spoons in open champagne bottles keep the bubbles

It is a myth that a silver spoon/fork left in the neck of a champagne bottle preserves its fizz. There is no scientific basis to this French folk tale.

why do goldfish have such limited memory spans

Research has shown that fish have a memory span of at least three months, including goldfish. The three-second memory belief is just an urban myth.

? does coke contain, or did it ever contain, cocaine

'Coke' is simply an abbreviation of Coca-Cola. The drink used to contain tiny traces from the coca plant; it is a myth that it contained actual cocaine.

? are daddy longlegs poisonous

Neither crane flies (better known in the UK as daddy longlegs) nor harvestmen (known as daddy longlegs in the US) contain venom that is dangerous to humans.

? why do your nails grow after death

They don't. After you die, your body starts to dry out and shrink, creating the illusion that your hair and nails are still growing after death.

? does milk help you sleep

You'd need 37 glasses of milk to have enough L-tryptophan to aid sleep. Turkey for sleep is a myth too. Relax. Read a book instead of tossing and turning.

can you answer these?

If you've caught our previous books, you might have had a go at the few odd questions we couldn't answer. Thanks for all the help on those, by the way. Now for some more, some imponderables that despite searching, digging, and rustling, we just can't find the answers to. Can you help? Answers straight to hello@aqa.63336.com please. Right answers get a special edition T-shirt.

Before you get on to these, a final, fond, farewell text. Do please save 63336 in your phone for when you're stuck in a tight spot, and visit www.aqa.63336.com to sign up to the AQA Club – you can explore other brilliant answers and it doesn't cost you a penny.

what is 14 bh in an os (excluding the b)

i live for centuries, but i do not move, i change moods as much as a woman... what am i

'nothing could be a bit of somethin': what's the song

who invented french cricket

what is the origin of the saying 'death is but a part of life'

why does bobby mcferrin not wear shoes

do pedestrians get right of way on a wall

why is 60 in darts called bagpuss

how many expressions are there for referring to someone leaving the door open, eg 'were you born in a barn'

wot is skinlagin

index